LIFE

The Journey to Eternal Joy

P. WESLEY STUBBLEFIELD

PAGE PUBLISHING
Conneaut Lake, PA

First originally published by Page Publishing 2023

ISBN 979-8-88654-654-5 (pbk)
ISBN 979-8-88654-655-2 (digital)

Printed in the United States of America

INTRODUCTION

The journey of life and its purpose have been the prime discussion throughout history and to this day. While others have given some insight that serving God is our objective, it is still unclear if devoted worship, absolute obedience, or living by the rules and lessons of God is the only explanation of our existence. In the same essence, many believers think everyone's fate has already been predestined long before our birth. That our religious convictions or our effort to become a good and loving individual plays no part in determining where we end up in the afterlife. That the Lord has already deemed those worthy to make it to heaven, and those He will send to hell.

The problem is these two conflicting ideas have been challenging for us human beings to figure out life's purpose and its destiny. One moment we believe God planned everything that happens on earth. And the next minute we question why He is allowing evil to manifest in the world? Especially, when it is against His will, and He has the supreme power to stop it. With no clear or definitive answer, some people resolve to disbelief while others rely on their faith and hope for the best.

You have heard the expression, "the truth is the opposite." And it is often used to point out contradictions within our religious belief. In this book, we will not only point out the discrepancy within our precision of the truth, but we will also disclose the conflicts within our mindset, within our culture, within our social behavior, and how they are undermining us human beings' happiness.

The good news is the message in this book clarifies and answers so many questions commonly asked like: why did God create heaven? If heaven was not enough, why did He create the earth? What is the purpose of life on earth? What is the purpose of the spiritual world? What is the benefit of eternal life? What is the root cause of sin? And how did we human beings inherit sin from Adam and Eve? And it tells the "life" story of Christ from a prospective that is eye-opening and will amaze you, the reader.

Furthermore, this book exposes Lucifer's deceptive behavior, his motive for misleading the first man and woman, and it reveals how his deceptions are pushing us human beings in the opposite direction and further away from God's purpose.

With that said, God is always working to bring clarity to these confusions irrespective of these setbacks. And history reveals He has been using men and women to steer us human beings in the right direction since our first ancestors derailed from the original plan. Because of His incredible work, the world has become more loving, more caring, more relational, more advanced, and more united than ever before. And the scriptures tell us God will continue to do so until His purpose for creation becomes a reality. It is within the same spirit this book simplifies the truth that is already known and shares a brighter light on the journey of life. Like I said before, this book intends to clarify life's purpose and how everyone is made to enjoy life forever. That means who you are today, you will always be. Not for five million or five trillion years, but forever. Let that sink in for a minute.

THE ATTRIBUTES OF GOD

The truth is God is love: He is beautiful, He is eternal, He is faithful, He is a spirit, and His plan for life is unchanging. In the same way, God created us human beings out of love. We are made to love, made to be loved, made to last forever, and that, too, will not change. However, when it comes to God's invincibility, His life is far greater than we currently know.

For example, the holy books tell us "God made the heavens." But as we explore this truth further, it becomes evident that God must have dwelled somewhere else, or He must have lived in a different realm before He created heaven. That is, for God to make heaven, He must have resided or existed outside of heaven before it was created. And that special place is superior, unique, and distinctive to God only. By knowing this critical piece of knowledge, it gives us human beings a deeper perspective about God, His life, the spiritual world, the universe, and our relationship with Him. With that being said, let us explore the creation of heaven and earth.

The beginning of God's creation

The beginning of the Creation started off with God's creation of heaven, as stated. This special place is magnificent in every possible way. To elaborate, according to Christ, the streets are made of gold, and there are many mansions in this spiritual realm to make the afterlife enjoyable. However, God's joy, by itself, could not be substantiated without someone to share it with. In other words,

God needed relational partners with whom to share His invention. For this reason, He created the angels to celebrate life and to make every occasion superb. In addition to that, God appointed Lucifer as the leader to substantiate His love in this new environment.

The Bible tells us Lucifer was the Daystar and the ruler who made every celebration pleasing to the Lord back then. No one went to God without going through Lucifer first.

Nevertheless, after a long period of enjoying "life" in the spiritual realm, maybe one hundred billion or ten trillion years later, it was clear that God needed to expand toward something new, bigger, and evolutionary for a better experience to enjoy *life* more. But instead of molding another spiritual sphere, this time God decided to create a physical world (Genesis 1:1) to also be as advanced, pleasant, and extremely beautiful.

The physical world is different and magnificent

The truth is the physical world is different, and it is made on another level. As you will later discover, it is further advanced than the spiritual world in many ways. The oceans' sunsets are picture-perfect, the mountains are touchable—even the low valleys are flood with fields of nectar to bring human beings joy. To describe it any other way will be an injustice to God's ingenuity.

However, due to this new world being physical, someone from the spiritual realm would need a physical body to enjoy the pleasure of the physical world. That means God would also need a physical body as His dwelling place and vessel to appreciate His latest invention. For this reason, He created us human beings in His image and as His temples.

With that said, it is important to acknowledge that human beings are made just like God. And everything we desire to be happy; God structured and embedded those characteristics within our nature for His and our pleasure as well. In other words, God made us that way to bring Him joy.

As stated before, God is love, and He wants love to be reciprocated. In the same way, we human beings live to love and to be loved in return. God appreciates beauty, and He lives for the joy of this amazing world. Likewise, we human beings desire the finest things of world to be happy and return that joy to God at the same time, its life purpose.

Unfortunately, the world becomes acclimatized to dis-associate God from pleasure, wealth, and the luxury of this amazing world. And this contradictory mindset is instigated by the devil to prevent us from enjoying our lives and denying God the pleasure at the same time. As mentioned early, we were made as His temple and dwelling place for that purpose.

God spirit dwelling in human being is no longer secret

The truth is God's spirit dwelling in us has no longer been a secret for many decades now. And people all around the world have come to the realization that the human body is made for His joy. Furthermore, it is important we emphasize how the identical physical body is also made as the dwelling place for the human spirit's pleasure as well. And this special ability is given to everyone for exploring and enjoying the physical universe forever just like God Himself; it's the key to life's eternal joy.

With that said, God's eternal attribute is an essential part of His being. For this reason, whatever He makes to enhance His life must also be structured and designed to last for eternity, even if it is in the physical form.

For God to achieve this vision within us human beings and the creation, He manifested His masculine and feminine attributes into separate characteristics. In other words, God displayed His masculine image into male and His feminine image into female. And this division of His image in the carnal form is structure to allow for the multiplication and expansion of the physical universe forever.

For example, us human beings multiply and evolve from a reciprocated relationship between a man and woman. Animals maintain their existence and keep expanding because of the male and female interaction. Also, atoms, molecule, and particles' functions improve only through the attraction relationship between the positive and negative charges. This relationship is unique to God, and it is what enables the physical world to last forever.

However, when it comes to us human beings, we are created with both physical and spiritual bodies. For this reason, it is necessary that both man and woman must first go through a process of spiritual growth to develop into God's likeness, to inherit His character, and to mature into his or her own individual identity. In this way, a man and woman would first replicate God's unique image in the physical form before reuniting into one body just as God is one. And this reunion is done through their holy matrimony.

Upon achieving this successful milestone in marriage, a husband and wife can begin to reproduce their own lives through their children and extend their family to create an eternal legacy. As stated before, this would be their eternal dwelling place in the physical universe like us human beings are to God. To paint a better picture of this wonderful lifestyle, here is an illustration of Sydney's joyful life story.

Sydney's joyful life story

As a young girl, Sydney grew up in profound family, and money was never an issue. Her parents provided all she could possibly dream of and more. Even though Sydney's family was wealthy, she was always kind, friendly, and treated everyone with respect. When her neighbors needed assistance, she was always eager to help. On many occasions, she would also provide her classmates with financial aid when needed.

One day, at her high school basketball game, Sydney and her schoolmates were singing and cheering their team on. As everyone harmonized, her friends began acknowledging that Sydney had an amazing voice. The team captain said she sings like an angel while others claimed that she was beautifully in a lane of her own. In response, Sydney agreed that music was her passion, and she was looking forward to being a part of a girls' singing group someday. Immediately, two of her friends offered to join, and that was the beginning of Sydney's fabulous music career.

At their graduation celebration, the group left the audience stunned with a jaw-dropping musical performance, and the community took notice. Luckily for the girls, one of the biggest music producers was at the graduation ceremony. He, too, loved their presentation and instantly signed the group onto his recording label. Within a few months, the trio released their first album, it was a hit, and the teenagers became superstars overnight. From Dubai to Tokyo, London, Paris, Australia, Africa, and so on. Everyone was talking about these new celebrities, and that was just the start!

As the group's popularity grew, so did their bank accounts. Within a short time, the girls had enough money to buy and enjoy the finest things life has to offer. In addition to their wealth, kings, prime ministers, and even presidents wanted to be entertained by this group. Nonetheless, despite Sydney's fame and fortune, she continued her love for God and treated the fans as she wanted to be respected.

Keep in mind: Sydney understands as a woman, she plays a profound role to establish a family. And her having children was a significant part of her life purpose to enjoy the universe forever.

During one musical award ceremony, Sydney was approached by another megastar that had a longtime crush for her. At first, she felt reluctant about this guy. For the simple facts, he appeared to have the bad-boy image—none of which Sydney wanted within her future family. But deep within, a small, quiet, and familiar voice asked her to give him a chance. So she did, but with caution.

After a few months of dating, Sydney was astonished by this guy's amazing personality. He was kind, caring, honest, funny, respectful, trustworthy, hardworking, and dedicated. But most of all, Sydney appreciated her man's love and the way he treasured everything about her. From then on, it was evident God had prepared this straightforward guy for Sydney. Her parents loved him—so did the fans throughout the world. Everyone anticipated their beautiful marriage commemoration.

As expected, the wedding ceremony took place on an exotic island with many superstars and celebrities from around the world. During the festivities, Sydney stunned the crowd with a powerful and heartfelt poem. And it signified the essence of a woman preserving her virginity until marriage.

She explained, "A woman is the mother that brings life into the universe. Her presence is the beauty which exemplifies the flowers, roses, and the fragrance of the earth. Everything is made from and through her. For this reason, her sexual organ is the perfect soil upon which the seed of life is planted. Therefore, it is holy! Glorifying! Dignifying! Honorable! Noble! And righteous! She remains unadulterated for her husband. To induce another man's seed on such ideal soil before marriage contaminates it and limits the potential of what God could have built for two people. For this reason, the Bible says to refrain from sex before marriage." Then she turned and looked directly into her groom's eyes.

"To my husband, I am that dignified woman who has remained steadfast for this glorious day. My purity is my greatest wedding gift to you. Tonight! We will begin to build a beautiful family destined for our joyful and endless future." Then she kissed him, and the audience applauded.

"Thank you!"

"These two together will become one powerhouse."

The guests congratulated the couple and proclaimed that these two together will become a powerhouse in the music industry. Whenever they performed, every concert was sold-out with more fans standing outside, hoping to get a glance at the couple.

Within two years of marriage, Sydney and her husband welcomed their first daughter. Everyone loved little Suzan, and she, too, became a princess to the world overnight. After four more years, a boy and another girl were added to the family. Nonetheless, the couple's passion for music remained steadfast and loyal as they continued to entertain their fans.

When Sydney and her husband were not working, you could catch the family cruising along the coast of France on their luxury yacht, spending summer vacation on their private island in the Caribbean, or perhaps enjoying winter skiing in the Colorado mountains.

No matter what the occasion may be, Sydney had the money to live her best life. And cherishing those intimate moments with her husband and kids were priceless. The reality is God who dwelled in the couple. He, too, was enjoying those precious moments through the family's lifestyle; it's life purpose.

After being in the music business for many years, Sydney eventually retired at eighty-seven to spend more time with her family traveling the world and making every occasion a memorable experience. By that time, the couple has had eight children, thirty-one grandchildren, and forty-two great-grandchildren, many of whom followed in their parents' career path as musicians. Others became sports athletes, air pilots, engineers, software designers, doctors, scholars, etc. Like any other parent, Sydney's greatest accomplishment and her proudest possession on earth was her family. As she stated, "My life's journey on earth could not have been any better. And I pray the Lord will grant me the same privilege to enjoy life better in the next world."

The truth is that Sydney and her husband were not two different or ordinary individuals. From God's perspective, they both resembled Him as one body for a much greater purpose. And that is to create their own eternal happiness. But let's get back to her life's story.

Sydney passed into heaven

When Sydney turned 101 years old, she passed into heaven to begin her next life's chapter as designed by God. Upon arriving in the spirit world, Sydney was flabbergasted with the delightful welcome from the elites of this amazing world. Wherever she was taken, the party was held in her honor. And she entertained the audiences with her amazing musical talent as well. To Sydney's surprise, her voice sounded more spectacular than it did on earth.

As the celebration continued, Sydney noticed everything in this new world had a distinct beauty. Not only were they stunning, but they were instantly responding to her every emotion and thought in mind. For example, when she walked in the garden, the flowers were putting out every fragrance she anticipated, and the grasses were immediately restored in their original form after she strolled across the lawn. Furthermore, when she finished swimming in the pool, the water quickly rolled off her skin and stayed completely dry as it was before the swim. There was no need for a towel. Even more fascinating, the DJ was playing every music that came to her mind without a request.

After a few surprising moments in the spirit world, Sydney came to the realization that whatever she wanted, it only required a simple thought in mind and suddenly, it was there. Unlike the physical world, time was not a restriction for her dream to become a reality. For Sydney, it was a world to die for, and she was glad to be a part of it.

When the celebrations gradually started transitioning into tranquility, the memory of her family and the pleasure of the physical world became desirable. Sydney wanted to see and spend time with her grandchildren. By then, it had already been another 150 years in earthly time, and her family lineage had expanded all over the universe. Sydney had kids in Africa, America, Asia, Australia, Europe, South America, and even on planet Mars.

Because of Sydney's massive family expansion, her life had just become more captivating. That's because time and space were no longer barriers for her to enjoy these different locations. In other words, Sydney could descend into multiple continents, dwell in several grandchildren, and pleasure in the same things they were enjoying without the restriction of time and space.

One moment she could be dining at one of the finest restaurants in Dubai, Tokyo, or Bora Bora. And the next minute she could be exploring the African safari in Tanzania or discovering the beauty of Mars. This is the benefit of a couple's offspring. It gives the parents' spirits the ability to enjoy life in the physical world forever just as they did in their previous life on earth. The good news is that this spiritual lifestyle is not limited to the rich and famous, but it is for everyone. And the key to this incredible life journey is achieved in the couple's bloodline.

Woman is the most essential person within marital union.

With that being said, the woman is the core individual within a marital union to substantiate a family happiness in the physical world and the spiritual world. That is, the woman leads the process to create lives, to extend the family lineage, and to advance the universe.

In fact, apart from what God has created, everything else that is invented or manufactured by us human beings is made possible through a woman. From the car we drive, the clothes we wear, and the houses we live in—these were all designed, fabricated, and built by someone born from a woman. Even our own lives were developed through women. The truth is that women will continue to take front stage for us to reach our full potential and for God's vision to become a reality in the universe.

To be clear, I am in no way suggesting that women are better or greater than men in any form. Nonetheless, the female role performed to validate God's purpose for our happiness is so significant, and it is worth mentioning and deserving of credit.

The good news is that our human lives are structured in such a spectacular way that it gives everyone the best of both worlds, including God Himself. Just as God planned to enjoy the creation through His children for eternity. In the same way, human beings can enjoy the universe forever through our family's lineages. This is the reason why children are called a blessing.

But then the question awaits, "why did Lucifer not see things from God's perspective?" Why did he spiritually kill God's children? Why did he tempt Eve first instead of Adam? How did he cause the couple to produce children of death instead of life? And how is he still preventing human beings from achieving *the* happiness as God intended? The truth is that the answers to these questions go further back prior to God designating Adam and Eve as ruler of the universe.

Adam and Eve, the king and queen

After a long period of God and the angels pleasuring in the spiritual world, as mentioned before. It was time for God to advance to a newer environment and something different to enhance life's joy. So He created the physical world.

But instead of God choosing Lucifer to rule the new world. This time He appointed Adam king and Eve queen, as His leaders. Then He blessed them with the ability to create as many lives as possible of their own (Genesis 1:28)—this capability Lucifer did not have.

In addition, God fashioned the couple's bloodline to expand and increase endlessly from one planet to another, which Lucifer did not have. But even more impressive, God's new king and queen were not only created with physical bodies, but also were made as spiritual beings. That meant Adam and Eve and their offspring would later transition into the spirit world. And they would continue to pleasure in the physical universe simultaneously, without limitation and forever. And that made Lucifer feel inferior and envied Adam's role.

From his perspective, God had given the first man and woman a more prominent status within His creation, and their positions would eventually make them rule both the spiritual and the physical world. For this reason, Lucifer came up with a plan to destroy the couple's ability of achieving that goal. And the only possible way he could make that happen is by contaminating their blood with evil deeds. So he seduced Eve into a sexual relationship. In other words, Lucifer transmitted his evil seed into Eve, who was the foundation of the couple lineage. This sin is what the Bible refers to as the forbidden fruit.

It was not a coincidence Lucifer tempted Eve first

It was not a coincidence that Lucifer tempted Eve first. He knew she was the core and the pathway for God's vision to be substantiated in the physical world. In fact, Lucifer understood that infesting Eve with his seed would cause the couple to reproduce children with his sin. And that would give him authority over her offspring. It is for this reason the scripture says we are children of the devil, we are all dead, we fall short of the glory of God, and it is within our desire to do devil's will. But then the question becomes, is sexual relationship between humans and spirits possible? The answer is yes!

That being the case, us humans having sex with spirits may seem unusual, unheard of, and perhaps, it may be difficult for most people to understand. However, it is not uncommon in many parts of the world. In fact, an American celebrity recently wrote about his sexual encounter with a spirit. In addition to that, the Bible and Qur'an mentioned angels having sex with us human beings (Jude 1:6–7). Besides, in the scene depicted in the Garden of Eden indicated Lucifer, Eve, and Adam's sin were sexual. But don't take my words for it. As the saying goes, a picture states the facts in thousand words.

The truth is Adam and Eve were naked in the Garden of Eden before the fall, and they were not ashamed of their nakedness. However, after they sin, the couple became embarrassed of their private parts. Not only that, but they concealed the area of transgression by hiding their sexual area. Clearly, this picture depicts Adam and Eve sinned with their private parts, which was the root cause of sin.

But do not get me wrong. I am in no way suggesting sex is bad or evil, nor is it against the will of God. On contrary, sex is the fundamental act that fulfills God's purpose for life. That is, sex create lives that are made to love, lives that are made to be love, lives that are made to expand love, and lives that make love last forever. For this reason, sex is called making love. *However, before a couple* can pleasure in this sacred act, both man and woman must first inherit God's characteristics or be like Him as mentioned before.

What we must acknowledge as human beings is that God forbids sex before marriage because it is detrimental to the human spirit. It can harm a couple's bloodline, and it can ruin the foundation for God to build a family for two people's eternal happiness. Even more damaging, the sexual relationship between Lucifer and Eve was never a part of God's plan. Satan was never designated to initiate such intimate relationships with us human beings, and God never intended for him to be our father. In spite of these setback, God plan for the creation has never changed. That means God will fulfill His purpose for creating us human beings, as stated in Isaiah 46:10–11.

> I make known the end from the beginning, from ancient time, what is still to come. I say: My purpose will stand, and I will do all that I please. From the east I summon a bird of prey; from a far-off

land, A man to fulfill my purpose. What I have said, that will I bring about; what I have planned, that I will do.

But the bad news is that Lucifer envy for Adam, his desire to overshadow him, and his desire to be first was transmitted to human beings. And this evil character is visible on every level in our human relationships. It can be seen between two powerful nations globally, between two bosses within an organization, and between two older brothers, even within royal families. Even worse, some people go to the extreme, causing physical harm or even death to achieve their goals, just as Lucifer did to Adam.

As you will later discover, this evil conduct undermines human development, prolongs God's effort to save the world, and not to mention, it could destroy humanity if we are not careful enough. The Reverend Dr. Martin

Luther King refer to selfish desire as the "The Drum Major Syndrome," and it is the worst kind of sin.

Lucifer and Adam; sons of God

The truth is Lucifer and Adam were both sons of God. And Lucifer was the first man God created, the first man closer to His heart, and the first leader He chose as an essential part to fulfill His purpose. In other words, Lucifer being the bigger brother, it was necessary he assist Adam and Eve to become their best to advance God's vision for the physical world. Unfortunately, Lucifer's failure to not recognize God's dream in this manner was a crucial blow to God's happiness and us human beings' pleasure as well.

With that said, God needed to change this negative narrative between two brothers to reinitiate the pathway to fulfill His purpose for us human beings. As mentioned before, God's plan does not change. For this reason, restoring the first and second sons' relationship was God's focal point for salvation and for us humans to enjoy life forever.

Jesus, the new Adam

The Lord could no longer use Adam directly

The reality is that God could no longer use Adam directly for restoration; sin was within his blood. That being the case, God needed a new Adam whose blood was pure, whose blood could wash away sin, whose blood could defeat the devil, and whose blood could begin a new "life" in the world. It is for this reason the scripture called Jesus the second Adam (1 Corinthian 15:45–47), the beginner of new life, the King of kings, the first and the everlasting, the savior, the Messiah, the father, the Christ, the conqueror, the prince of peace, the living Word, the Word made flesh, the son of God and the list goes on (Luke 1:31–33, 9:20; Matthew 3:17).

Just as all things were to begin through the first Adam, the same was true for Christ. All things were made through him, and all things are to be fulfilled in him. However, for God to breed the second Adam, He had first to restore the failure of His two sons, as mentioned before. And that rebuilding process began within Adam's first and second sons, Cain and Abel.

Cain was first, just as Lucifer was, and Abel was second, representing Adam. These two brothers were the focus for God to lay the groundwork to save us human beings from sin. Unfortunately, Cain murdered his younger brother, Abel (Genesis 4:8), just as Lucifer killed Adam. And that was just the beginning of Lucifer's identical evil character repeated in our human history.

The struggle between two brothers

The truth is that this struggle between the two brothers continued in many of God's selected families for thousands of years until Esau and Jacob broke the circle. That means Isaac's two boys brought the victory God needed to advance His work of salvation from the family stage to the national level. In other words, God's work to rebuild the first and second sons' bond was successful in Isaac's family. And their achievement created the foundation for God to continue His work in a nation of people. It is for this reason Israel is called the chosen nation.

To be clear, Esau and Jacob's bond was not an overnight success. The Bible tells us the two boys fought throughout their childhood. Even more astonishing, Esau wanting to kill Jacob was consistent with Lucifer and Cain's motive for killing their younger brothers.

But as God would have it, Esau overcame his temptation and recognized Jacob as the chosen one. Upon their family's triumphant victory, God blessed the two men. And Jacob was anointed to breed the Jewish lineage and the second Adam, who is Christ. It is for this reason Jacob is called the father of Israel.

With that said, Israel had to also triumph over this identical and selfish desire for God to advance His work to the global stage. And evidence shows the struggle between two brothers was apparent in many Jewish families, even as far back into the mother's womb (Genesis 25:23).

But then the question becomes, why did it take hundreds or even thousands of years for God to select a family or a chosen nation to restore Lucifer and Adam's failure? The answer is simple. Just as time was required for Adam and Eve to inherit God's attributes, time is necessary for

God to remove Lucifer's evil from within us human beings' blood. And the longer the failure repeats itself, the more time will be needed for God to advance His work.

Next question: what is the significance of having two brothers to initiate God's vision in the physical world? The truth is everything that God creates to improve, increase, or advance, it must function and operate within a pair system. In other words, it takes two engaging within a reciprocal relationship for all things in the creation maintain their existence, increase and last forever.

The fact is that we human beings are created with both physical and spiritual bodies. It was the imparity of the leaders of these worlds to establish the link of love for us human beings to enjoy life in these two worlds forever. In other words, their union was the key to establishing the foundation for everyone to embody and encapsulate both the spiritual and physical attributes fully. For this reason, restoring the spiritual and physical bond for us human beings was an essential part of God's plan to save the world.

With that being said, John the Baptist and Jesus were Israel's two finest sons anointed by God to conquer this evil. And their union was essential to begin God's kingdom of heaven on earth, just as it was for Lucifer and Adam in the past. Even more significant, John came first, and he was anointed as the primary person to reveal Jesus as Christ to the chosen nation. And this responsibility was critical for Israel to recognize Christ and for us human beings' salvation.

The Life story of Jesus
John the Baptist and Jesus

As stated, John the Baptist was the firstborn. And the Bible tells us he was mighty in spirit, and the miracles surrounding his birth spread throughout the nation of Israel. Furthermore, John lived in the desert, surviving only on locusts and honey. Everyone listened to him because of his sacrificial lifestyle; even the chief priests came to John for baptism. In fact, John was so highly respected that some people thought he might be the Christ. In a way, God made the Jewish people put their faith in John, so that John would make the chosen nation believe in His son.

On the other hand, Jesus's birth was very simple compared to John's. He was born second, just as Adam. His birth took place in a manger, and very few people knew about the holy signs surrounding his childbirth. Nonetheless, Jesus was destined to be king and preordained to begin *a new life* into the universe. The truth is Jesus's role was more powerful and far more significant than John's. Yet and still, John was the key person to make God's vision a reality through his little cousin Jesus; they were family.

John and Jesus grew up in the spirit of the Lord

The Bible also tells us both John and Jesus grew up in the spirit of God. However, John did not know his little cousin Jesus was the Christ; it was not yet revealed. Fortunately, the time came for God to expose His son to the world. For this reason, Jesus went to be baptized by John.

Immediately after the baptism, the clouds of heaven opened, and John saw the Holy Spirit descending upon his cousin Jesus. Right then, the voice of God spoke and said to John, "This is my son. In him, I am well pleased" (Matthew 3:16–17).

It was official; *the Christ* has been unveiled to John. From then on, it was John's responsibility to proclaim the son of God on every hill, on every mountain, and in every valley throughout the entire Jewish nation. At first, John did not hesitate, but immediately testified to the crowd at the Jordan River. "This is the one whom I said would come after me. He is the lamp who takes away the sin of the world." However, what John did after his initial pronouncement is mind-boggling.

The Bible tells us John did not follow Jesus; he did not continue to proclaim Jesus to the religious leaders, nor did he declare Jesus as the Christ throughout Jerusalem. Instead, John went his separate ways and left Jesus to announce himself as the Messiah to the chosen nation.

When was John asked why was he not working with Jesus? John responded, he must increase, and I must decrease (John 3:30). John's answer contradicted God's prophecy and was the opposite of his mission to pave the way for Christ. With this evidence, it was clear something wrong must have been going on in John's mind, and that riddled the Jewish people.

The truth is God decreases no one working for His purpose. On the other hand, He always has advanced, increased, blessed, and prospered those closer to His heart, especially His leader on the frontline. How could it have been any different for John? Why did he not want to increase with Jesus?

It was obvious: John going his separate way confirmed he envied Jesus's role just as Lucifer did to Adam. Even worse, John questioning Jesus if he was really the Christ clearly demonstrated his doubts for Jesus and his loss of faith in God's revelation at the Jordan River. For that reason, Jesus did not waver but condemn John as the least in the eyes of God. But do not take my words for it. Here are Christ's words from the scriptures stating the facts.

Now it came to pass, when Jesus finished commanding His twelve disciples, that He departed from there to teach and preach in the cities.

And when John had heard in prison about the work of Christ, he sent two of his disciples and said to him. Are you the coming One, or do we look for another?

Jesus answered and said to them, go and tell John the things which you have hear and see. The blind sees and the lame walk, the lepers are cleaned, and the deaf hear, the dead are raised up and the poor have the gospel preached to them.

And blessed is he who is not offended because of me.

As they departed, Jesus began to say to the multitudes concern John. (Matthew 11:1–7)

For this is he of whom it is written: Behold, I send my messenger before your face who will prepare your way before you.

Assuredly, I say to you, among those born of woman, there has not risen one greater than John the Baptist; but he who is least in the Kingdom of Heaven is greater than he.

From the day John until now, the kingdom suffer violence and violent men take it by force. (Matthew 11:10–12)

It was clear that the devil had once again undermined the second Adam just as he did the first one. And this decline in God's plan made it difficult for the Jewish people to accept Jesus's proclamation of himself as Christ. As mentioned before, it was John's job.

The good news is that Jesus had already overcome, conquered, and defeated the devil on a personal level. In addition, he had inherited "the life" and the second Adam's role. None of which Satan could change, prevent, or take away. In other words, God's son had established kingship on Earth for the first time in human history. However, it was still necessary for the Jewish people to believe, accept, and have faith in His son for human beings to receive the benefit; they were the chosen nation.

Faith in Christ was the key for human beings' salvation

Just as faith in God's word was required for Adam and Eve to inherit life initially. In the same sense, faith in Christ was the key for human beings to receive new life. With that in mind, Jesus was determined to find faith in Israel, even if he had to walk the pathway alone.

At first, the people welcome him, and the crow came by thousands. The sick were cured (Matthew 17:14–18, Luke 8:43–48), the blind could see (Mark 8:22–26, Matthew 20:29–34), and the dead were brought back to life (Luke 8:49–56, John 11:38–43). With things heading in the right direction, Jesus was optimistic about the future of God's kingdom. For this reason, he asked his disciples to pray for God to send more help.

That's until the spiritual leaders realized the rapid growth of Christ's ministry was a threat to their positions. Therefore, the lawmakers would not allow anyone to express their faith in Jesus or follow him, and that was the beginning of his trouble.

The Pharisees and lawmakers accused Jesus of falsely declaring himself as the Messiah, for the simple fact that his testimony did not fall in line with the scripture—it was

John's mission, as stated before. Furthermore, they accused him of committing blasphemy, being possessed by a demon, and not to mention breaking the law of the Sabbath. Long story short, Jesus was condemned for claiming to be the son of God. And according to their law, he must be put to death. And that was the motive of the crucifixion, the opposite of God's will for His son.

Clearly, the discrepancy between God's two prominent leaders in Israel led to the killing of His son once again. And that error prevented human beings from being truly free from sin and receiving "the life" from Christ just as it did for the first Adam. For this reason, Jesus must come again and give us a second chance to life.

But then the question becomes, wasn't it predicted that Jesus was going to the cross and died for our sins? Yes, it was prophecy, and it is written all over the scriptures.

However, what is not emphasized is that God also predicted that Christ would be accepted, he would give new life to the world, all governments would be upon his shoulder, there would be no end to his kingdom, and the list goes on.

The reality is God has always given two opposing prophecies. One regards us human beings' faith in the *Word*, and the other is for our disobedience. In other words, if we human beings have faith in the world, then we would receive life and prosper. On the contrary, if we disobey the word of God, then we would be cursed and suffer.

Unfortunately, Jesus (THE WORD) was rejected, and many religious leaders automatically concluded Jesus's crucifixion was God's will because it was predicted. Even though it is written in the scriptures that is further from the truth. Once again, here are Christ's words stating the fact:

> I told you that you will die in your sins; if you do not believe that I am the one I claim to be, you will indeed die in your sins.
>
> Who are you, they asked? Just what I have been claiming all along… (John 8:24–25)

> I know you are Abraham's descendants. Yet you are ready to kill me because you have no room for my word.
>
> I am telling you what I have seen in the Father's presence and you do what you have heard from your father. Abraham is our father, they answered. If you were

Abraham's children, said Jesus, then you will do the things Abraham did.

As it is, you are determined to kill me, a man who has told you the truth that I heard from God. Abraham did not do such things.

You are doing the things your own father does. (The devil) We are not illegitimate children, they protested. The only Father we have is God Himself.

Jesus said to them, If God were your father, you would love me, for I came from God and now I am here. I have not come on my own; but he sent me.

Why is my language not clear to you? Because you are unable to hear what I say. You belong to your father the devil, *and you want to carry out your father's desire.* He was a murderer from the beginning, and not holding to the truth, for there is no truth in him. (John 8:37–47)

If you, even you, had only known on this day what would bring you peace but now it is hidden from your eyes. The day will come upon you when your enemies will build an embankment against you and encircle you and hem you in on every side. They will dash you to the ground, you and the children within your walls. They will not leave one stone on another, because you did not recognize the time of God's coming to you. (Luke 19:42–44)

These scriptures have been in the Bible for over two thousand years. However, many religious leaders skip over or neglect them because they cannot explain the difference between the two prophecies. But, as the saying goes, there is more.

None of the ruler of this age understood it, for if they had, they would not have crucified the lord of glory. (1 Corinthian 2:8)

Was there ever a prophet your fathers did not persecute? They even killed those who predicted the coming of the Righteous One. And now you have betrayed and murdered him. You who have received the law that was put into effect through angels but have not obeyed it. (Acts 7:52–53)

The son of man will go as it is written about him. But woe to that man who betrayed the son of man! It would be better for him if he had not been born. (Mathew 26:24)

Matthew 23:13–39: the seven woes of the Bible. Please read these verses in its entirety for a deeper understanding.

Woe to you, teachers of the law and Pharisees, you hypocrites! You shut the kingdom of Heaven in men's faces. You yourself do not enter, nor will you let those enter who are trying to… (Matthew 23:13)

At the end of this speech, Christ turned to children of Israel and said the following:

O Jerusalem, Jerusalem, you who kill the prophets and stone those sent to you, how often I have longed to gather your children together, as a hen gather her chicks under her wings, but you were not willing.

Look, your house is left to you desolate.

For I tell you, you will not see me again until you say, blessed is he who comes in the name of the Lord. (Matthew 23:37–39)

Then they ask him, what must we do to do the work God requires? Jesus answered; the work of God is this: to believe in the one he has sent. (John 6:28–29)

Jesus said, my kingdom is not of this world. If it were, my servant would fight to prevent my arrest by the Jews. But now my kingdom is from another place.

You are the king, then! Said Pilate. Jesus answered, you are right in saying I am a king. In fact, for this reason I was born, and for this I came into this world, to testify to the truth. Everyone on the side of truth listen to me. (John 18:36–37)

The essence of faith

The truth is, having faith in God's word is the most essential part of His plan to work through us human beings. It was required for Him to free the Israelites from Pharaoh, it was required for Him to bless the chosen nation, and it is needed for Him to save the world from sin. Without it, nothing is possible.

Furthermore, every progress or achievement we human beings have made was because of one man or one woman's faith. It was Abraham's faith that reinitiated the relationship between us human beings and God (Genesis 22:15–18). Then it was Moses's faith that freed the children of Israel from pharaoh (Hebrews 11:24–29). Jacob's faith established the Israelites' blood of covenant with God (Genesis 28:10–22). Esther's faith saved the Israelites in exile (Esther 4:16), Ruth's faith initiated the bloodline for Jesus (Matthew 1:5–6), and Jesus's faith opens the door of life for us human beings to be truly free from the devil (John 10:9).

Here are few words of wisdom to help us all grasps the true essence of faith.

Faith attracts God to you
Faith makes God work for you
Faith makes God to bless you
Faith is the essence of life
Faith attracts life
Faith restores life
Faith strengthens life
Faith brings hopeful
Faith brings freedom
Faith makes salvation possible
Faith illuminates the
pathway to joy

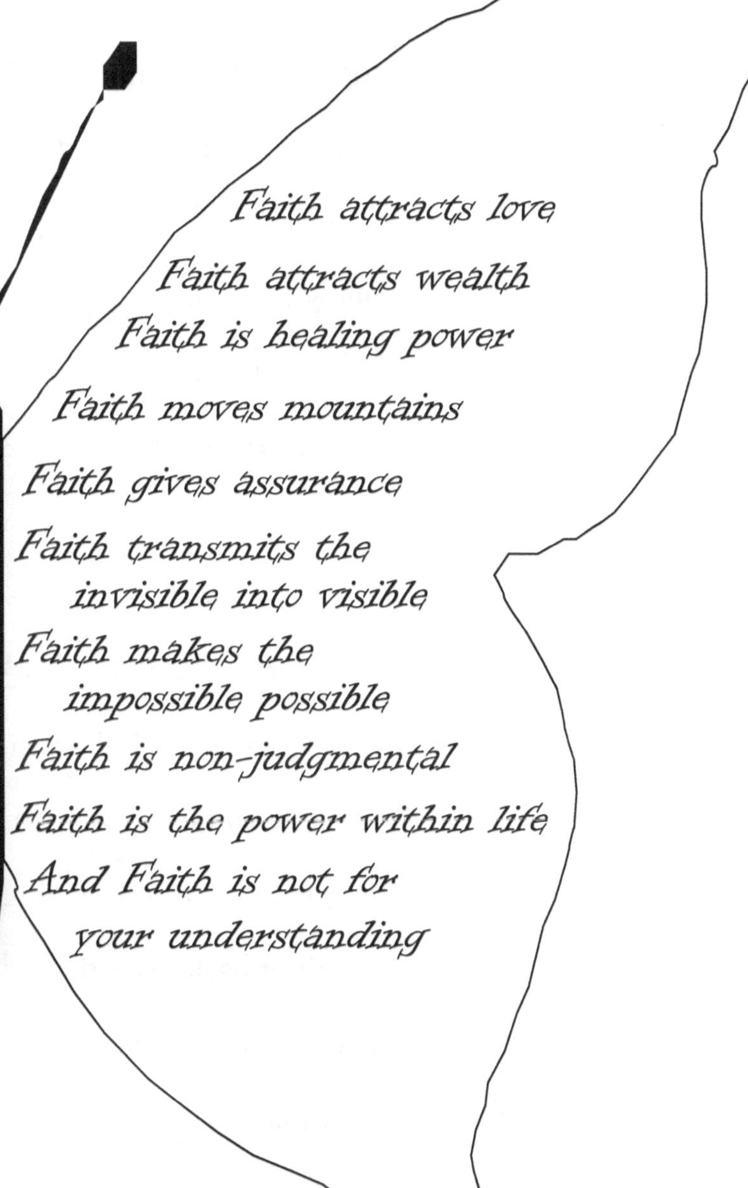

Faith attracts love
Faith attracts wealth
Faith is healing power
Faith moves mountains
Faith gives assurance
Faith transmits the
    invisible into visible
Faith makes the
    impossible possible
Faith is non-judgmental
Faith is the power within life
And Faith is not for
    your understanding

Christ's determination to find faith in Israel

As mentioned before, Christ's determination to find faith in Israel was second to none. That is if the Jewish nation would not accept him as the son of God. Indeed, his disciples believe he is the coming one. If not all twelve of them, maybe three would follow him, or perhaps one would stand by him to the very end even if he must die to do so. This level of faith God requires of Jesus, and the same was true for the disciples.

On the other hand, Jesus knew such a level of his disciples' faith in him would only lead to life instead of death. For the simple fact, God is a God of life and not death. For this reason, Jesus stated to his disciples. "He who is willing to lay down his life for me would gain it back instead. And who is willing to save his life will lose it" (Matthew 16:25). And evidence shows Abraham and many others of God's champions exemplified such a level of faith in the past that defeated the devil.

For example, God asked Abraham to sacrifice his only son as a burnt offering. Interestingly, Abraham made no complaint, nor did Isaac refuse to be the sacrificial lamb. As Abraham proceeded to slaughter his son, God intervened and said to him, "Do not lay your hands on the boy, and now I know you have faith in me."

The excellent news is Abraham's faith gained his son's life back; he became the father of Christian and Muslims, and his seeds are spread throughout the world as an eternal reward for his faith. The reality is that God did that much for Abraham's faith back then. How much more He could have rewarded Peter, James, John and the other nine disciples if they had remained faithful in Christ?

What us human beings need to realize: God may require a person to demonstrate his or her faith to the point of death. However, His plan is not to seek that individual's death. On the contrary, God's intention is to prove that person's faith in Him supersedes the fear of death. For that reason, God always rewards such level of faith with life, wealth, and much more. With that being said, Jesus needed to encourage the disciples to follow him at all cost, including their own lives. Once again, Jesus's words from the scripture:

> Then Jesus turned to his disciples, if any-
> one would come after me, he must deny
> himself and take up his cross and follow
> me. For whoever want to save his life will
> lose it, but whoever loses his life for me
> will find it. What good will it be for a
> man if he gains the whole world, yet for-

feits his soul? Or what can a man gain in exchange for his soul. For the Son of man is going to come in his Father glory with his angels, and then he will reward each person according to what he has done. I tell you the truth, some who are standing here will not taste death before they see the Son of man coming in his Kingdom. (Matthew 16:24–28)

Greater love has no one than this, that he lay down his life for his friend. You are my friends if you do what I command. I no longer call you servant because a servant does not know his master business. (John 15:13–14)

The only way one could defeat evil is, he or she must be willing to die to con-quer it.

Jesus took Peter, James, and John on the mountaintop

As Jesus continued to further strengthen his disciples' faith, he took Peter, James and John to the mountaintop. Upon arrival, Christ transfigured with his clothing becoming bright like the sun. Just then, Moses and Elijah appeared, speaking to him. As their conversation continued, a bright cloud developed, and then the voice of God spoke to the three disciples.

"This is my son, whom I loved, with him I am well pleased. Listen to him" (Matthew 3:17).

Once again, God had confirmed that Jesus is His son. But this time, it was to Christ's three most devoted followers. With their own eyes, they saw Jesus standing together with Moses and Elijah, and with their own ears, they heard the voice of God's validation that Jesus is His son. Even more significant,

Jesus took it one step further and warned Peter, "The devil has asked to test you. But I pray your faith will not fail."

Reason being that Peter's faith could have been the final attempt to defeat the devil if necessary. For this reason, the scriptures also confirm that Peter was the rock and foundation upon which Christ intended to build his house or his Father's kingdom on earth.

As the final hour slowly approached, Christ gathered the twelve disciples as his last effort to reaffirm their commitment. Then he said to them:

"This very night you will all forsake me, yet I would not be alone."

In response, Peter said, "Even if all fall way on account of you, I never will."

"Really, Peter?" Jesus said, "Will you lay down your life for me? This very night before the rooster crows, you will deny me three times."

But Peter declared again, "even if I must die with you, I will never disown you. And all the disciples said the same" (Matthew 26:31–35).

Keep in mind that Christ's prediction of Peter's denial was a prophecy and written in the scripture. However, Peter had a choice. And the right one was to believe in him whom He had sent. That was God's expectation of him, and the same was true for Christ.

Finally, it was time for the disciples to validate their faith, so Jesus led them into the Garden of Gethsemane. As for Peter,

James, and John—the three most faithful ones—Christ took them a little farther into the garden and said to them:

"My soul is overwhelmed with sorrow to the point of death. Stay here and keep watch over me" (Matthew 26:38).

Then Jesus proceeded a slight distance, bowed his face to the ground, and began praying.

"My Father, if it is possible, may this cup (death) be taken away from me. Not as my will but as your will" (Matthew 26:39).

The Bible tells us that Jesus did not offer this prayer once, but three times, asking God to remove the cross from his pathway.

But then, why did Jesus not prefer going to the cross? The answer is obvious. It was not God's will. Also, Jesus understood that going to the cross would not free human beings from sin. It would not free the Jews from the Romans' oppression. Moreover, it would not establish God's kingdom on earth in his lifetime, as predicted in the scripture.

In addition, Jesus knew that going to the cross was a fundamental sacrifice, and the only alternative to giving human beings a second chance to life. With that being said, everyone knows that second chances are given only after the first process has failed, and that is the case with the cross.

The bad news is that Jesus knew that his death on the cross would cause Jerusalem to be destroyed. It would cause the Jews to be persecuted, enslaved, imprisoned, and tormented in foreign nations. Moreover, it would cause human beings' relationships to spiral downhill, which would lead to more suffering. That means that there would be senseless wars, poverty, genocide, bigotry, sex trafficking, greed, more slavery, and many other evil crimes that are prevalent in today's world.

For these reasons, Jesus prayed to continue preaching the truth and to save the world from the tragic future ahead. But let us continue with the story in the Garden of Gethsemane.

When Jesus returned to his followers for the third time, he found them sleeping again. This made it evident that the disciples could not substantiate the faith that God needed to free the world from sin. So, Jesus proclaimed:

"Are you still sleeping? The time has come, and the son of man has been abandoned into the hands of sinners. Rise up! Here comes the enemy" (Matthew 26:45–46).

As expected, Jesus was detained and taken to the chief priests for an interrogation. Upon arrival, the lawmakers flogged him, spat on his face, and tortured him for claiming to be the son of God. From a distance, Peter stood and watched. To make matters worse, he denied Jesus three times, claiming:

"I never knew the man" (Matthew 26:69–75). Once again, the scripture was fulfilled.

However, did Peter rejoice for obeying the scripture? Absolutely not! On the contrary, Peter wept bitterly because he did not fulfill God's will, which was to believe in His son.

The bottom line is that Jesus did not find faith in Israel. No one was willing to lay down their life or stand by him in the final hours. As a result, God had to sacrifice His only begotten son to give us a second chance to life. In the end, Christ was taken to Pilate, the Roman leader who had the final saying to authorize the crucifixion.

Pilate's interrogation

Pilate then went back inside the palace, summoned Jesus and asked him, "Are you the king of the Jews?"

"Is that your own ideal," Jesus asked, "or did others talk to you about me? Am I a Jew?" Pilate replied, "It was your own people and chief priests who handed you over to me. What is it you have done?"

Jesus said, "my kingdom is not of this world. If it were, my servants would fight to prevent my arrest by the Jews. But now my kingdom is from another place."

"You are a king then," said Pilate.

Jesus answered, "You are right in saying I am a king. In fact, for this reason I was born and for this reason I came into this world, to testify to the truth" (John 18:33–37).

Upon hearing those words from Jesus, Pilate's assessment found no evidence of Christ deserving death for the charges against him. Furthermore, Pilate knew it was out of envy and jealousy the Jewish leaders sentenced Jesus to death. So he reproached the lawmakers in Jesus's defense. Once again, the scripture speaks:

> Once more Pilate came out and said to the Jews, look, I am bringing him out to you to let you know that I find no basis for a charge against him. When Jesus came out wearing the crown of thorns and the purple rob, Pilate said to them, here is the man! As soon the chief priests and offi-

cial saw him, they shouted, Crucify him! Crucify him!

But Pilate answered, "you take him and crucify him. As for me, I find no basis for a charge against him."

The Jews insisted. "We have a law, and according to that law, he must die because he claimed to be the son of God. (John 19:4–7)

It is clear that Jesus was crucified for claiming to be the Christ and this was the opposite of God's purpose.

With that being said, God has always been able to turn evil into good, or at least find a pathway to save His children even in their disobedience. Christ dying on the cross was for that purpose. In other words, God sacrificed His son's life as ransom, and a price paid to buy human beings back for a second chance to "life."

> But I tell you the truth: it is for your good that I am going away. Unless I go away, the counselor will not come to you. When he comes, he will convict the world of guilt in regard to sin and righteousness and judgment. In regard to sin, because men did not believe in me. (John 16:7–8)

All written scriptures are not the will of God

The truth is all written scriptures are not the will of God. Just as God's words are printed in the holy book to educate His children, He also writes warnings about the devil's intentions to mislead human beings. Unfortunately, our inability to differentiate between the two led to the confusion of us believing that Jesus's crucifixion was the will of God. I must admit, I too was on the opposite end, until I began questioning this explanation of the cross as early as the fourth grade.

If I did not mention this before, I am from Liberia, which is the most faithful Christian nation on the planet—at least, so I think. In this West African, and American colony, Christianity was taught in every grade level. From kindergarten and throughout high school, the Bible was a major part of our culture and part of the syllabus in the school system. Passing its course was a requirement to be promoted into the next class. In addition, the government required all businesses to remain closed during Sunday morning worship services. Even circular music was forbidden on radio stations until 6:00 p.m.

For me, Sunday afternoons were always the most enjoyable time for Christian activities planned around the city.

The Youth for Christ and Youth Crusaders were my favorites. We played games, ate, received toys, and watched religious movies for the most part of it. During each festivity, the teaching that Christ came to die for our sin remained steadfast throughout the celebration.

On one occasion, the celebration for Christ was held for elementary and junior high school students at the Monrovia City Hall auditorium. The program included musical performances, stand-up comedy, religious drama, and of course, a movie to complete the event. The movie selected this time was *The Crucifixion*.

During one section of the film, the religious leaders began brutalizing Christ, and that scene became unbearable for a female student sitting a few rows in front of me. As the lawmakers intensified the punishment, her screams became louder and louder. Eventually, she was escorted out to maintain calmness in the auditorium.

Me, being led by my curiosity, I followed to see why she was weeping so passionately. Especially when the crucifixion was the exact will of God. Back then, it did not make any sense to me, and for a long time, that event bothered me. Today it is cleared that the crucifixion was the manifestation of evil unfolding before her eyes. And for that reason, she could not help but cry. Which brings us back to God's plans to reveal His son to the chosen people.

God's effort to reveal His son

The truth is that God made every effort to reveal His Son to the chosen people. To facilitate the process, He put into place religious customs and traditions. And one of those was the requirements for each Jewish family to offer the firstborn son as Levi to serve God in the temple. That means Jesus, who was Mary's first son, was also destined to work in the temple as Levi.

In retrospect, if Mary had done so. The religious leader would have recognized Jesus's spiritual power at an early age and acknowledged that he is the Christ. And this would have automatically eliminated the possibility of the people's disbelief and Jesus going to the cross. Jesus made it clear to his mother, Mary. "Don't you know I am supposed to be in my Father's house" (Luke 2:49)? Sadly, Mary ignored this religious custom and lost the opportunity for her son to be recognized by the lawmakers.

Another missed prospect was God's prediction that David's seed would remain on Israel's throne forever. As usual, faith was required in God's instruction for David's lineage to make that prophecy a reality. Therefore, if David's sons had obeyed God's prerequisite to not intermarry with foreign nations, Jesus would have been born into royalty. Presented as a king, he most certainly assumed his kingship without resistance from the people; he is the son of David. Unfortunately, Solomon's disobedience caused David's bloodline to lose the throne.

Finally, God assured the Jewish people that He would send Elijah back before the coming of Christ. This, too, was an important landmark all Israelites awaited. In fact, on every Sabbath, a chair would be placed in each Jewish household anticipating Elijah's arrival.

Once again, God kept his promise and sent John the Baptist to fulfill Elijah's role. Even more significant, Jesus confirmed John was Elijah (Matthew 11:13–15). Regrettably, John denied he was (John 1:21). That, too, added more confusion for the people to identify and accept Jesus as the Christ.

The bottom line: God's entire efforts to reveal His son to the chosen people ended up in failure. Solomon disobedient, the Jewish people's failure to carry on their religious custom, and John denied he was Elijah. In the end, Christ was rejected, and the devil's desire to kill the second Adam was fulfilled just as he did to the previous one. For that reason, a second chance was necessary, and it is for this purpose Christ is coming again.

In the next topic, *The devil's deception*, we will uncover Satan's deceit and how he continues to prevent us human beings from becoming our best. It is my hope these revelations give us all the faith and the willingness for the truth to open the pathway to "life." Keep in mind, the truth has always been within us. And it only takes the *Word* to confirm and apply it, even if it is challenging.

The devil's deceptions

The devil's deception has been the most challenging thing to pinpoint or identify. That's because he gives the opposite of the truth to make believe his doing is the will of God. And for the longest time, this has been his trick to deprive and steal us human beings' happiness. What is even more devious: the devil's motive for his deceit is often never related to the conflict in question or the subject of his deception.

For example, it is evident the black race is the origin and the parent of us human beings. That means everyone in the world came from the black people. Not only that, but all talents, skills, knowledge, wisdoms, strength, and emotions God intended for humankind were embedded into the black race.

With this truth, it would seem proper that black people are treated with respect for being the first ethnic group and the central line for God to produce us human beings. Regretfully, blacks are neglected, persecuted, exploited, hanged from trees, and murdered like animals in the streets because of their skin color.

But the reality is that the devil's ultimate motive for suppressing black people is not about skin color. It is because God engrained all life's attributes, characteristics, and talents He intended for us human beings into the first human race. Unfortunately, the devil created the false impression that the black color is no good, it represents him or evil, and that reversal of this truth is only intended to drive us human beings in the opposite direction and further from God's purpose.

On the contrary, the color black is powerful; it is diplomatic, it represents professionalism, it is elegant, it is bold, it symbolizes wealth, it is classic, it induces luxury, it is durable, it is sophisticated, it is good, and it produces light. Furthermore, black is required for all other colors to have depth and variation, which is valid with the black race. In other words, God made the first human beings black as the depth and the foundation to reproduce all other races. With this truth, it is clear the black color is a vital part of God's ingenuity. And it plays a distinctive role to produce different qualities and traits of His creations, including life.

In fact, the Bible tells us God created light out of darkness. In other words, before there was light, God existed in complete darkness. And evidence shows everything cultivates better in the dark. Life grows healthier in the dark, social activities are more pleasurable in the night, lovemaking is nicer in the dark, even many of us human beings were conceived in darkness.

But then the question becomes: why did Satan select the black color to represent him or evil? The answer is clear. Black color is valuable, attractive, and it plays a significant role in God's creation and us human beings' creativity as well. Furthermore, the color black amplifies life, it enhances us human beings' joy, it existed with God in the beginning, and it is the original color of love. For these reasons, the devil induce himself into the black color to prevent us human beings from inheriting all the attributes of blackness.

The evil imposed on black people does not hurt them alone

What we must realize: the evil imposed on black people does not hurt them alone. On the contrary, it deprives everyone from receiving significant contributions this exceptional group of people could have made.

However, do not get me wrong. I am not suggesting black people are superior or supreme to other races. Nevertheless, they have been the trailblazer to enhance social lifestyle and improve healthcare despite their four hundred years of oppression. To be clear, black people invented vaccination, pioneer music, transformed sports, promoted space exploration, and built the most powerful nation called the United States on earth.

With that being said, it is crucial black people are given equivalent partnership on the global stage for the world to reach its full potential. In retrospect, if black people had equal rights like everyone else, the world would have been further advanced and a far better place. That was God's plan for us human beings from the beginning and the same remains true today.

Human beings are special creatures

The truth is us human beings are made with special abilities and with gifts unlike other creatures. That is, we are designed as spiritual beings, created as God's temples, and made as the family dwelling places. In addition, each person is made distinctly, with unique skill and talent only he or she can contribute to the world.

That being the case, the evil perpetrates on one individual hurt everyone, including God. In other words, by disallowing one person his or her basic rights to survive, in the same way, it is denying God the privileges to rightfully experience His joy through that person, it is depriving that person's ancestors to enjoy the world through him or her, and it ruins the possibility for everyone else to plea-sure from the contribution that person could have made, including the perpetrator.

The good news is we are just at the beginning of life's eternal adventure, and our unity is the key for us human beings to undo the past mistakes and for us to better enjoy life as we advance from one universe to another. That means there will be newer planets unlike the earth in many ways. These new worlds will have spanking color arrangement, outstanding cultures, better lifestyles, and more beautiful colors of people. Unfortunately, the belief that life is too short is another trick from the devil. And this opposite mindset is preventing many people from planning for life's eternal joy.

Woman plays the central role for life's eternal joy

As mentioned before, women play the central role to create lives, expand life, increase the family lineage, and to enjoy life forever. For this reason, God intended women to outnumber men to make this family dream a reality. Sadly, God's plan to have more than one woman expand a family bloodline has been misconstrued, wrongly interpreted, and twisted from its original purpose. And this misconception is one of many of Satan's deceptions that is preventing the world from achieving life's maximum potential of Joy.

With that being said, the ratio gap discrepancy between men and women is not coincidental. God did not make an error by producing fewer men than women. He did not mean for some women to marry and others not. He did not plan for some women to have their own families and others not. Unfortunately, the conventional marriage of one woman to a man is causing an imbalance in our love relationships and social instability.

As a result, many women are prevented from experiencing the love of a husband and the privilege to have children for their eternal future. Furthermore, this problem also denies countless children from sharing the love from both parents, the love of a father, and in some cases, also from a mother. And research shows that children lacking these types of relationships are likely to abuse drugs, involve in crime, join gangs, engage in prostitution, and participate in everything else that undermines society's peace and stability.

It is clear, the current marital standard is causing many men to divorce their wives, abandon their children, and not to mention that others have murdered their entire families only to fulfill the desire of another woman. In addition, the problem is declining the tranquility of life, and it causes more grief in the world than the happiness the rule anticipates.

On the other hand, us men's aspiration to have more than just one woman is embedded within our DNA. It's explicit, it's persistent, and this desire has been unstoppable even though our tradition states otherwise. You have heard the expression, "all men cheat."

But then the question becomes, is it a coincidence that all men cheat? Or were they built, designed, and created that way for a bigger purpose? The answer is obvious. God fashioned men with that ability for a good reason. And that is to expand the family lineage for everyone to enjoy life better in the physical world forever.

The truth is "children are a blessing" and God's greatest gift to a family. And the greater the number, the larger the blessing. For this very reason, women outnumber men in a more excellent ratio.

When God blesses a family, it is also for the household to create many temples so that He, too, may enjoy what they are enjoying.

With that being said, this change may be complex and challenging because of how further the devil has led us in the opposite direction. On the other hand, we human beings must fully encapsulate God's purpose of creation, and that He will not change. That means allowing all women to be a part of a family. To experience the love of a husband, to experience the joy of having children, and to take part in the pleasure of life's eternal happiness. Furthermore, all children must experience the pleasure of being in a family, sharing the love of both a mother and a father. It's God's purpose. And the sooner we adapt to His standard, the brighter our lives will become. As mentioned before, God's purpose does not change.

For there is always light, if only we are brave enough to see it, if only we are brave enough to be it.

—Amanda Gorman

A man having more than one wife is nothing new

The truth is, a man having more than one wife is nothing new, and it is not a foreign idea either. In fact, having multiple wives was a better part of the Jewish culture to increase the family descendants. Furthermore, God has been working in such family structure to breed His hero, birth His spiritual leaders, and to advance His vision for the world

For example, Jacob, the father of the chosen nation, had multiple wives and was the key to the birth of the Jewish lineage. What is also true: God made no distinction regarding the children's motherhood, nor did He reject any of the siblings because of their moms' position in the marriage. On the contrary, God accepted Jacob's twelve sons, with each one representing one of Israel's tribes.

The same was true for David and many of God's other champions. Even more impressive, Jesus is the son of God. He, too, came from the bloodline of the other woman. The reality is that God had used multiple women in the past to increase His family lineage. He can certainly do the same today for us human beings to expand our families' heritage. In other words, if it was not a sin back then, it is never sin ever. That's because God's plan does not change, nor does He dwell or work in sinful activity. Speaking of sons, they are an essential part of God's plan to increase a family bloodline.

The family lineage is carried on in the sons

The Bible tells us God created Adam as His son. Through Adam's blood, He multiplied "life." It is through Adam's blood that His purpose for life would be fulfilled, and the same is true for a father. Through his son, the family seed is planted on Earth, and through his son, the family lineage would expand from one planet to another for eternity. In fact, scientific research confirmed that the family seed is carry-on only through the son. And the more sons a father has, the bigger and greater access a family would have in the internal universe. For this reason, God designed women at a more excellent ratio than men.

The critical understanding in this matter. A man having multiple wives is not one size fits all, and God structuring women to outnumber men does not mandate every man to have multiple wives. In fact, some men cannot handle multiple women, and few can hardly keep up with a single wife in his household. That means having multiple wives is a choice, and the family willingness to financially support a huge family for their eternal future.

Even more significant is the wives' readiness to establish a loving relationship amongst themselves. Without it, the family will not stand, and the aspiration to create a bigger and better family lineage will crumble. Furthermore, the plan to have multiple wives in a family is never determined by the husband but his wife.

The reason is that the woman is the producer of life, the patron of love, the children's educator, and the family's financial brain. She can foresee which woman would better develop and increase her family bloodline. In other words, a man's success is determined by his family lineage, and the woman is always the key to that achievement.

What is also true, the lineage established by the husband benefits everyone within the marital union. That means the bloodline created by Mary is also the lineage of Esther, Sandra, and their husband. This is God's plan to make a family enjoy every aspect of His vast creation in the forever.

If you really want to know how rich you are, find out how many things you have that money can't buy.

—Riky Rick

The reality is everyone would be living in the spiritual world at point in life. And each person would want to spend some time with their family and to experience the pleasure of the physical universe. And the only pathway to fully encapsulate such joy would be in the family lineage. This is the spiritual lifestyle people often referred to as "coming back to life," but it is that and more.

The beauty of the spirit lifestyle

As mentioned before, the spirit world is unique and beautiful, with distinct characteristics. And one of its prime attractions is that the human spirit is not limited by time and space, nor is it restricted to one individual. That means a spirit person can find pleasure in several people, in multiple locations, and have different experiences at the same time. This identical attribute is also embedded within God, and it is what enables Him to be everywhere simultaneously and to enjoy every aspect of His creation. There is no end to this spiritual lifestyle, and it is fascinating.

Imagining life's eternal journey

As I imagine life's eternal journey, I am captivated by the new worlds God is creating for our future. Instead of seeing another blue and green planet, I am entranced to experience life on a pink and purple planet. Unlike the earth, the raindrops, landscape, oceans, and sky reflect the same shade. Even more impressive, the average temperature is seventy-five degrees year-round—it is never too hot or cold.

Furthermore, the vehicles are nothing compared to any cars seen today. As seen in science fiction movies, they travel to hilltops, fly to low valleys, and quickly land on yachts. When it comes to intercontinental flights, the aircraft travel from one continent to another within an hour, while interplanetary trips take a couple of hours. As for the food, it is not worth mentioning because your mouth might get watery. But you get the picture.

The truth is us human beings' perceptions of life's pleasure are just the tip of the iceberg and the beginning of countless and much more significant things to come, and women are the keys to exploring it all.

CONCLUSION

As I conclude, I must briefly talk about sex and a few other things the devil is still using to destabilize us humans' happiness. Yes, I said sex. It is sacred. It is beautiful. It makes love, produces life, increases the family's lineage, and the joy from this divine experience is second to none in the universe.

Because sex is still essential for human beings' development, the devil has also created the false impression that it is ungodly and nasty. And this negative perception is driving us human beings further from God's purpose. And for the most part, people are ashamed to embrace it or talk about it. But the bad news is that this negative mindset is instigating premature sexual relationships and destroying the possibility for God to produce the lineages He intended for many families' eternal happiness.

Even worse, countless men and women permanently sacrifice sex, believing they are doing God's service, but that is further from the truth. The reality is sex is the core of life and the pathway for our human being's eternal happiness. It cannot be sacrificed, nor can it be altered or neglected in one's lifetime. Even more significant, God commands us human beings to temporarily hold off on sex for spiritual development and physical maturity, but He never meant it to be a lifestyle.

With that being said, a sacrifice is always specific, and the condition surrounding one is changeable depending on the individuals or the community of people. Furthermore, a sacrifice is usually made as an offering to draw closer to God, made as restitution for sin, or it is made to better other people's lives.

Unfortunately, the devil creating an opposite impression for sex is a classic example of him depriving us the things meaningful to life. And that includes the most pleasing people who sacrifice their lives for us human beings.

Neglecting our sacrificial men & women

For example, the brave men and women of the military are surrendering their livelihood, giving up their families, sacrificing their lives, and fighting for our peace, freedom, and happiness. Instead of us reciprocating the same services for these respectable soldiers, most are deprived of life's necessities, while others are left homeless on the streets. Even worse, many brave men and women are not given proper healthcare to heal the pains and injuries sustained on the battlefield. But it doesn't stop there.

We also see this mistreatment of our firefighters, our police, our teachers, and many other first responders. They are all placed at the bottom of the compensation list and underpaid. But here is the worst of all.

As mentioned before, women are at the pinnacle of everything God intended for us human beings. They produce life, extend the future, and they create life's eternal joy. Unfortunately, these good loving mothers have been treated like second-class citizens, isolated from the global development, and deprived of their fundamental rights to survive. Even the great United States was once guilty of this crime. The bad news is women are still being persecuted and mistreated today in many parts of the world for no reason.

It is undeniable that we have become people with a habit of doing the opposite by turning what is first into last. And it is stealing our joy, killing ourselves, and we do not even realize it. For this reason, the Bible says the first shall become the last, and the last shall become the first, and it is time to make these changes.

About the Author

P. Wesley Stubblefield is a man of God. Even though he works in the construction field, his calling to discover the truth has been a journey throughout his life. He has studied the Bible from cover to back several times and he has associated himself with many religions and Christian organizations.

In 2019, Wesley was inspired to share with the world these incredible revelations he discovered on this spiritual expedition.